# The Middle East

**David Scott**

### Consultants

**William O'Mara, Ph.D.**
*History Professor*
California State University, Dominguez Hills

**Brian Allman**
*Principal*
Upshur County Schools, West Virginia

### Publishing Credits

Rachelle Cracchiolo, M.S.Ed., *Publisher*
Emily R. Smith, M.A.Ed., *SVP of Content Development*
Véronique Bos, *Vice President of Creative*
Dani Neiley, *Editor*
Fabiola Sepulveda, *Series Graphic Designer*

**Image Credits:** p.10 (left) Flickr_Alfgrn; p.10 (top) Wiki Commons/Marie-Lan Nguyen; p.10 (bottom) Met Museum; p.13 (top) Fausto Zonaro; p.14 (bottom) Getty Images/Andrew Matthews–PA Images; p.15 (bottom) Getty Images/PA Images; p.16 (bottom) Alamy/Juliet Highet/Art Directors; p.16 (top) Shutterstock/The Road Provides; p.17 (top) Alamy/Reuters; p.17 (bottom) Alamy/Mark Reinstein; p.18 Shutterstock/Seyephoto; p.19 Shutterstock/Nur El Imany; all other images from iStock and/or Shutterstock

### Library of Congress Cataloging-in-Publication Data

Names: Scott, David (David Coleman), 1971- author.
Title: The Middle East / David Scott.
Description: Huntington Beach : Teacher Created Materials, Inc, [2023] | Includes bibliographical references and index. | Audience: Ages 8-18 | Summary: "The Middle East is a cradle of civilization. When humans first migrated out of Africa, they settled in this land. It was in the Middle East that the wheel was first invented. Farming was invented here, too. People now look to the Middle East to provide one-third of the world's oil. It is a beautiful land, rich in history, art, science, and culture"-- Provided by publisher.
Identifiers: LCCN 2022038216 (print) | LCCN 2022038217 (ebook) | ISBN 9781087695143 (paperback) | ISBN 9781087695303 (ebook)
Subjects: LCSH: Middle East--Juvenile literature.
Classification: LCC DS44 .S36 2023  (print) | LCC DS44  (ebook) | DDC 956--dc23/eng/20220816
LC record available at https://lccn.loc.gov/2022038216
LC ebook record available at https://lccn.loc.gov/2022038217

**Shown on the cover is Dubai,
United Arab Emirates.**

## TCM
### Teacher Created Materials

5482 Argosy Avenue
Huntington Beach, CA 92649
**www.tcmpub.com**
ISBN 978-1-0876-9514-3
© 2023 Teacher Created Materials, Inc.

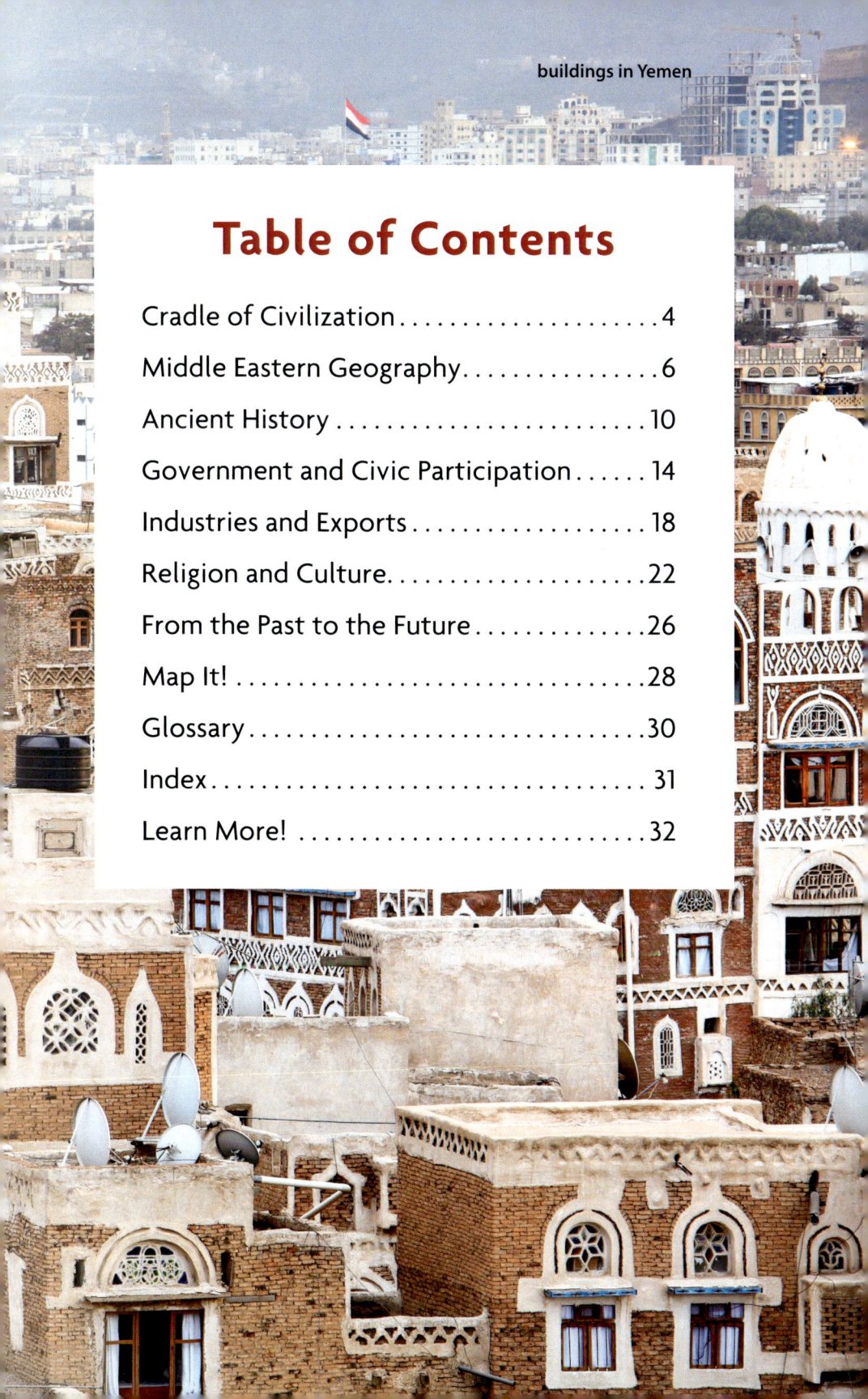

buildings in Yemen

# Table of Contents

# Cradle of Civilization

The land where Africa, Asia, and Europe meet is often called the *Middle East*. It is also known as West Asia. It is a land rich in history and **culture**. There are many **natural resources** in this region.

When humans **migrated** out of Africa, they first settled in the Middle East. The world's first civilizations grew from this area. For this reason, it is known as a cradle of civilization. Many cultures developed and spread from this area.

Hagia Sophia, Istanbul, Turkey

Alborz Mountains, Tehran, Iran

Black Sea

TURKEY

CYPRUS

SYRIA

*Mediterranean Sea*

LEBANON

PALESTINE

ISRAEL

JORDAN

EGYPT

Red Sea

*Some North African countries, including Libya, Algeria, Tunisia, and Morocco, can be considered part of the Middle East.*

Farming was invented in the Middle East. Many other inventions people use today come from this part of the world. And the Middle East is the birthplace of three major world religions. Many people make **pilgrimages** here during their lifetimes. People visit historic sites and ruins. Part of this region is sometimes called the *Holy Land*.

The Middle East is rich in history, science, art, and natural resources. It is a global power in world affairs. Middle Eastern culture has influenced the world in many ways.

**Saudi Arabian desert**

# Middle Eastern Geography

The population of the Middle East is more than 440 million people. And it continues to grow. More than 100 million people live in Egypt. Both Iran and Turkey have over 83 million people each. Bahrain and Cyprus have the smallest populations. Each country only has about 1 million people.

The Persian Gulf is an important body of water in the Middle East. It is sometimes called the *Arabian Gulf*. It connects to the Indian Ocean. It is a vital **waterway** that ships pass through to deliver goods. It is very important for oil tankers. Oil from the Middle East is delivered around the world. Those oil tankers start in the Persian Gulf.

oil tanker in Dubai

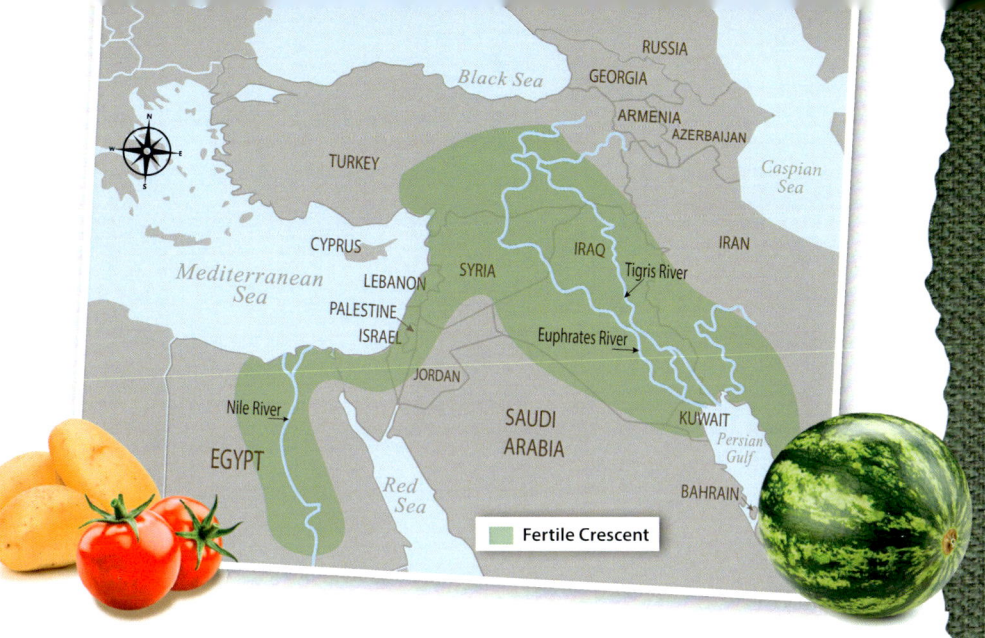

Fertile Crescent

One area of land in the region is famous for farming. The land along the Nile River and the Tigris and Euphrates Rivers forms a crescent shape. It is known as the Fertile Crescent. **Sediment** from the rivers creates rich farmland. This farmland begins in Egypt. It travels northeast along the coast. It goes all the way into Turkey. Then, it follows the river basin south into Iran and Iraq. Potatoes, tomatoes, and watermelon are grown here.

Water in this region is mainly used for **agriculture**. Water in this region is also used as drinking water. The crops grown in the Fertile Crescent help feed many people in the region. Some of the foods are even sent around the world. It is very important to keep the water clean. Water is valuable in this dry climate. Each country's government works to keep fertilizer and pollutants out of the water.

## The Silk Road

The Silk Road was an ancient trade route. It connected Africa with Europe and Asia. It was most used from 130 BCE to 1453 CE. Middle Eastern inventions, such as the toothbrush and hand cranks, were traded on the road. People were able to share religions with new areas thanks to the road. Parts of the road still exist as a paved highway.

Divers can explore the coral reefs in the Red Sea.

The Middle East has some of the largest deserts in the world. It also has some of the most beautiful beaches. The sands are white. The water is a pale blue. Some of the beaches are good for surfing. Others are good for snorkeling, fishing, and sailing. The Red Sea has beautiful coral reefs.

The Middle East also has important waterways. The Tigris and Euphrates rivers begin in the mountains of Turkey. They flow through Syria and Iraq into the Persian Gulf. The Nile River begins in Africa, and it flows north through Egypt. The Suez Canal is a 120-mile (193-kilometer) human-made waterway. It was built in 1869. It connects the Mediterranean Sea to the Red Sea.

Euphrates River, Turkey

Mount Damavand, Iran

It snows in some parts of the Middle East. The mountains of Lebanon, Iran, and Turkey are popular ski destinations. Israel also has a ski resort. Mount Damavand in Iran is the highest peak in the Middle East. It is also a volcano. It has hot springs and gas holes. It is still considered active! But, the last time it erupted was in 5300 BCE. Mount Damavand is popular with mountain climbers. Trout swim in the rivers there. Eagles fly in the sky. Juniper trees grow in the higher altitude. In spring, red poppies cover the foothills. Mount Damavand is a symbol of Iranian pride. It even appears on Iranian money.

## Second-Largest Desert in the World

The largest desert in Asia is in the Middle East. It is called the Arabian Desert. It goes through multiple countries. A large part of it is in Saudi Arabia. There is a wide range of elevation throughout the desert. There are vast plains, tall mountains, and steep canyons.

# Ancient History

The first humans migrated out of Africa. They were hunter-gatherers. Hunter-gatherers followed their food sources. They did not stay in one place for very long. But a group of these humans settled in the Fertile Crescent. Cows, goats, sheep, and pigs thrived in this region. The animals fed on the plants that grew there. They drank from the rivers and streams. The people settled in the area with the animals.

Farming began to develop in this area. This farming community was known as Sumer. It was settled between 4500 and 4000 BCE. Sumer was located in modern-day Iraq. The fertile soil in this area allowed people to grow crops. Ancient humans grew lentils, wheat, and chickpeas. They also grew fig trees. **Irrigation** canals were built. These delivered water to the crops. Images of farm plows have been found on ancient **pictographs**. Over time, the practice of farming spread across the world.

carving of a king-priest feeding a herd of animals from 3200 BCE

ancient clay tablet with depictions of malt and barley

**Sumerian princess figurine from 2150 BCE**

These ruins are of the city of Dara, one of the important Mesopotamian cities in Turkey.

## Mesopotamia

Sumer and other civilizations grew. The area where these civilizations developed became known as Mesopotamia. That means "between the rivers" in Greek. This refers to the Tigris and Euphrates Rivers. Over time, **archaeologists** have found many objects from these civilizations. This includes art, pottery, and tools. It also includes tablets with written words. Historians have been able to translate some of these. They have a better record of these early **dynasties** thanks to these findings.

### The Invention of the Wheel

It is believed the wheel was invented in Mesopotamia. One of the oldest wheels found has been dated to the 3000s BCE. It was a pottery wheel. Pictographs of wheeled wagons have been dated to this time period, too.

This map shows the land conquered by the Persian Empire.

# Persian Empire

The Persian Empire was actually several dynasties. They were in modern-day Iran and Iraq. The first was founded around 550 BCE. It spanned from Greece to India. It had one government. It included Mesopotamia and Egypt's Nile Valley. The Persians created the world's first postal service. They built many roads between Africa, Asia, and Europe.

# Byzantine Empire

The later Roman Empire is sometimes called the Byzantine Empire. For more than 1,000 years, it ruled over much of the Middle East. Its capital was the city of Constantinople in Turkey.

People pray in Mecca.

In 622 CE, the religion of Islam was founded. The prophet Muhammad founded it in Mecca. Mecca is a city in Saudi Arabia today. It is part of the Holy Land. In 634, **Muslim** armies began to fight against the Byzantine Empire. The empire lost the Holy Land. The Holy Land is the birthplace of Judaism and Christianity. It is also sacred to Islam. This land became united under Islam.

Beginning in 1095, armies from some European countries began a series of wars. These wars are called the *Crusades*. They were fights over the Holy Land. They lasted for hundreds of years.

## Ottoman Empire

The Ottoman Empire began in Turkey around 1299. In 1453, the Ottoman leader took over Constantinople. It was renamed as Istanbul. This marked the end of the Byzantine Empire. The Ottoman Empire took over. It ruled the Middle East for more than 600 years. This empire came to an end in 1922.

Mehmed II conquered Constantinople.

### Baklava

Baklava is a popular dessert in the Middle East. The word *baklava* dates back to the Ottoman Empire in 1650. This dessert is made by layering pastry dough. Chopped nuts and honey are put inside. Similar desserts have been made since 800 BCE.

# Government and Civic Participation

Some European countries took over Middle Eastern countries by force. This happened after World War I. After the takeovers, people started **revolutions**. They did not want to be controlled by other countries. They fought for their freedom. Iraq became independent in 1932. Saudi Arabia also became independent in 1932. Egypt declared independence in 1922. But Britain still had some control over the country. It was not fully independent until 1952. The United Arab Emirates unified and gained its independence in 1971. North and South Yemen came together as one in 1990. It became known as Yemen.

Each country now has its own government. The countries have constitutions. A constitution states the beliefs and laws of a country. It explains how a country is run.

Many countries in the Middle East have monarchies. A king or queen rules in this type of government. Royal families can go back many years. Bahrain has

first king of Bahrain

been ruled by the same family since 1783. The Al Thani family has ruled Qatar since 1868. Monarchies can also have prime ministers. These leaders serve under the monarch. A monarchy can have a parliament, too. This is a **council**, or a group of people who makes laws.

president of the United Arab Emirates with the monarch of the United Kingdom in 1989

## Emirates

The United Arab Emirates has seven emirates. An emirate is a division of land. It is like a state or a province. Each emirate is ruled by an emir. An emir is a male monarch or a prince.

People shop at a covered market in Oman.

A citizen is a person who has the full rights and protections of a country. Some countries allow people who are born in that country to become a citizen. But if they are not born there, it can be difficult to become a citizen. In Oman, it is rare for foreigners to become citizens. The person must live in Oman for 20 years. It can be brought down to 15 years if the foreigner is married to an Omani and has a child with them. There are other requirements, too. But being a citizen has its benefits. Citizens of Oman can receive free public healthcare. They also can receive free public education up to the secondary level. Some Middle Eastern countries have less strict rules. In Syria, it does not matter if a person is born there or not. They can become a citizen if their father is a citizen.

elementary school in Sur, Oman

People wait to vote in Lebanon.

Citizens in the Middle East have other rights as well. Voting is one of them. But not every country in this region has regular elections. Syria, Saudi Arabia, and Yemen do not hold elections regularly. Qatar held an election for the first time in 2021. Saudi Arabia sometimes has elections for its Federal National Council. All federal laws have to go through the council.

## The First

Tansu Çiller was a young and smart economics professor in Istanbul. In 1991, she became Turkey's minister of state for the economy. In 1993, she ran for prime minister. Several men ran against her. But she had a better campaign. The people liked her. Çiller became the first female prime minister of Turkey.

# Industries and Exports

Nearly half of the world's oil comes from the Middle East. Saudi Arabia alone produces twelve percent of the world's oil. There are several other oil producers in the Middle East. Iraq and the United Arab Emirates produce four percent. Iran and Kuwait both produce three percent.

Qatar has one of the world's largest natural gas reserves. It is the third-richest country in the world. Iran is also one of the world's largest producers of gas.

The Middle East produces more than just oil and gas. Turkey has the largest economy in the Middle East. Factories produce cars and construction materials. Agriculture is also important. Turkey is the world's largest producer of hazelnuts, cherries, figs, and apricots. More than 20 percent of people in Turkey have jobs in agriculture. Other crops, such as pomegranates, are grown in the Middle East, too. Turkey is a major supplier of clothing and other textiles. It exports around $14 billion in clothing each year.

Factory workers in Turkey make jeans.

A woman harvests cherries in Turkey.

Banking is another big industry in the Middle East. Bahrain is home to many large financial businesses. A large part of its business comes from the oil and gas industry. Many banks in Bahrain follow Islamic law. These are laws based on the Qur'an. The Qur'an is the Islamic holy book. One of its laws forbids banks from charging interest on loans.

Qur'an

## Limited Resource

Oil has many uses besides automobiles. It is also used to make plastic. Certain toys, clothes, and makeup are created with oil. But there is only a limited amount of oil on Earth. Other materials, such as plants, are starting to be used to make these items now.

Dubai

# Tourism

Another large part of the economy of the Middle East is tourism. Every year, more than 50 million tourists visit the region. In Egypt, people want to see the pyramids, the Sphinx, and the Valley of the Kings. Some of the pharaohs were buried in the valley.

In Jordan, people visit Petra. It is an ancient city that was carved into the side of a mountain. Tourists also like to float on the Dead Sea. The Dead Sea is a very large lake. It is located on the border of Jordan and Israel. The Dead Sea is almost 10 times as salty as the ocean. There is so much salt in the water that people can easily float on top of it.

Petra in Jordan

Dubai is a city in the United Arab Emirates. The tallest building on Earth is located in Dubai. It is 2,717 feet (828 meters) tall. This building also has the world's highest observation deck, swimming pool, and restaurant. The elevator travels 22 miles (35 kilometers) per hour! Even though it is that fast, it still takes about a minute to reach the observation deck.

## Palm-Shaped Island

Palm Jumeirah Island is a human-made island. It was made using sand and rock, and it is shaped like a palm tree. Now, it is home to resorts and beaches. A **monorail** transports visitors up and down the tree trunk in the middle.

# Religion and Culture

Many people in the Middle East are Muslim. Muslims follow the religion of Islam. Islam is an **Abrahamic** religion along with Judaism and Christianity. They all believe in the same God. There are nearly two billion Muslims around the world.

Saudi Arabia is home to Mecca. Mecca is the holiest city in Islam. It is the birthplace of the Islamic prophet Muhammad. Every year, millions of Muslims make a pilgrimage to Mecca. Non-Muslims are not allowed to enter Mecca.

At the center of the Great **Mosque** of Mecca is the *Kaaba*. *Kaaba* means "cube" in Arabic. It is the most sacred site in Islam. It is considered to be the house of God. It has existed since before the time of Islam. Tradition says that Adam and Eve were the first people to build a shrine there. It has been damaged and rebuilt many times since then.

the Kaaba in the Great Mosque of Mecca

the Blue Mosque in Istanbul, Turkey

There are five key practices in Islam. These are known as the Five Pillars:

1. There is only one God, and Muhammad is the Messenger of God.

2. Prayer happens five times a day while facing in the direction of Mecca. Muslims pray at sunrise, noon, afternoon, sunset, and night.

3. Charitable giving to those in need in their communities is required.

4. Fasting (no eating or drinking) happens during the daylight hours of the holy month of **Ramadan**.

5. A pilgrimage to Mecca should occur once during their lifetime. (This is only required if it is possible for the person to do this.)

## Diversity

Not everyone in the Middle East is Muslim. There are several other religions practiced in the region. Christians, Jewish people, and Hindus live in the Middle East. Languages in this region are diverse, too. Did you know that Arabic is not just a single language? There are several varieties.

# Clothing

People in the Middle East sometimes wear special clothes. A *thawb* is an ankle-length garment. It is similar to a robe. It has long sleeves. White is usually worn in summer. Black is typically worn in winter. A *bisht* is a cloak

This man wears a *keffiyeh*.

a man can wear over a *thawb*. A *keffiyeh* is a square scarf that covers a person's head. It provides protection from the sun. It can also cover a person's face and mouth to protect them from the wind.

A woman can also wear a *thawb*. A long cloak that a woman can also wear is called an *abaya*. A *hijāb* is a long scarf a woman can wear to cover her head and hair. If a woman is wearing a *niqāb*, it also covers her face. A woman can choose to wear a *hijāb* for many reasons. For some, it shows pride in their religion. For others, it provides **modesty** while in public.

traditional clothing in the Middle East

falafel

halloumi

manakish

# Food

Many flavorful dishes and foods can be found in the Middle East. Hummus is one popular food. It is a dip eaten with pita bread. The word *hummus* is Arabic for "chickpeas." Chickpeas can also be mixed with spices and fried into little balls. These are known as falafel.

Manakish is like a pizza. It is a round dough topped with meat, cheese, and spices. It is usually eaten for breakfast or lunch.

Halloumi is a type of cheese. It is made from goat and sheep milk. It does not melt. Halloumi can be used instead of meat in vegetarian dishes. It can also be grilled and eaten by itself.

## Halal and Kosher Foods

Muslim and Jewish religions have rules about what foods can be eaten. Food that is approved as halal or kosher will have small symbols on the packaging. If a food is marked halal, it is approved for Muslims to eat. Kosher foods are approved for Jewish people to eat.

# From the Past to the Future

One of the oldest places of worship in the world is located in Turkey. It is known as Göbekli Tepe. Around 9500 BCE, hunter-gatherers carved giant pillars that still exist. They carved them out of rock. They did not have any metal tools. At that time, pottery had not even been invented yet. At this spot, the pillars stand 16 feet (5 meters) tall and weigh up to 10 tons (9,071 kilograms). Images of scorpions, lions, and other animals are carved into the pillars. The bones of wild animals have been found nearby.

These people had not learned how to farm yet. Grinding stones found at the location prove they ate grain, such as the wheat that grows naturally nearby. Only five percent of this area has been excavated. That means there is still more for archaeologists to discover. Many remains of the past will soon be found there.

Göbekli Tepe

Jerusalem, one of the oldest cities in the world

Other remnants of the past can be seen throughout the Middle East. This land has been important to humans for thousands of years. And it still is. It is a beautiful land that is rich in history and natural resources. The Fertile Crescent offers abundant food and water. The Persian Gulf provides oil and gas to the world. The people of the Middle East gift the world with advancements in art, science, religion, and history.

## The Beginning of the Alphabet

**Turquoise** miners in Egypt invented an early system of phonemic writing. This happened around 4,000 years ago. They used only the first sound from Egyptian hieroglyphs. They scratched letters onto the wall of a mine. The letter *a* comes from *aleph*, meaning "ox." The letter *b* comes from *bêt*, meaning "house." They captured each sound from the language they spoke.

symbol for *a*

symbol for *b*

# Map It!

Much of the land in the Middle East is dry desert. Water is extremely important for life in this region. People, animals, and crops depend on it. Make a topographic map of the Middle East that shows the major waterways of the region.

1. Draw an outline of the countries in the Middle East, or start with a blank map.

2. Label the countries in the Middle East. Include the capital cities.

3. Research to determine the major waterways of the region. You'll want to find any notable rivers, gulfs, canals, and seas.

4. Draw these water sources on your map and label them.

5. Mark which parts of the land are desert and mountains.

6. Share your work with a partner. Did your partner have different water sources on their map? If so, add those to your map.

sailboats on the Nile River

coast of the Red Sea, Egypt

Tigris River

Euphrates River

Nile River

Red Sea

Tigris River, Iraq

Euphrates River, Turkey

# Glossary

**Abrahamic**—a type of religion, such as Judaism, Christianity and Islam, that follows the God of Abraham from the Book of Genesis

**agriculture**—the science of farming

**archaeologists**—scientists who learn about past human life by studying objects that ancient people left behind

**council**—a group of people who are chosen to make rules, laws, or decisions about something

**culture**—the beliefs, customs, arts, etc. of a particular society, group, place, or time

**dynasties**—powerful groups or families who rule over a country for a long time

**irrigation**—the method of supplying land with water by using artificial means (such as pipes)

**migrated**—moved from one place to another at different times of year

**modesty**—the quality of being moderate or avoiding indecency

**monorail**—a train that travels along a single rail or track

**mosque**—a building used for worship by Muslims

**Muslim**—a person whose religion is Islam

**natural resources**—materials supplied by nature that can be used by humans

**pictographs**—prehistoric drawings on a rock wall

**pilgrimages**—journeys to a special place, usually for religious reasons

**Ramadan**—the ninth month of the Islamic year, when Muslims fast from sunrise to sunset

**revolutions**—movements or attempts to overthrow current governments and start new ones

**sediment**—material that settles into land or water, usually made of rocks, minerals, or decomposed plant or animal life

**turquoise**—a bluish-green mineral used in jewelry and other objects

**waterway**—a river, canal, or other route that is deep and wide enough for boats and ships to travel through

# Index

dates

Dates grow on date palms.

# Learn More!

Many countries in the Middle East are ruled by a monarchy.  A monarchy is a form of government.  A king, queen, or emir rules for life.  Some families have ruled for generations and hundreds of years.  This is called a *dynasty*.  A dynasty is a series of rulers from the same family.

Make a family tree of a monarchy from the Middle East.

- Choose a country in the Middle East that has a monarchy.  Research its leaders.

- Write the current ruler's name at the left side of a sheet of paper.

- Work your way across the page by making branches for their parents.  Make note of which ones were rulers.  Be sure to write the years they were born and died.  How many generations back can you go?

Dolmabahçe Palace in Istanbul, Turkey